USBORNE ROUND THE WORLD IN FRENCH

With Easy Pronunciation Guide

Carol Watson and Katherine Folliot
Illustrated by David Mostyn

Pronunciation guide by Anne Becker

En ville

l'église

le garage

la maison

le jardin public

l'arrêt d'autobus

les feux de signalisation

le passage clouté

l'affiche

le panneau indicateur

l'hôtel

l'usine

le magasin

la cheminée

le garçon de café

la caserne de pompiers

la voiture de pompiers

4

E. Bell.

First published in 1980
Usborne Publishing Ltd
Usborne House
83-85 Saffron Hill
London EC1N 8RT
© 1989, 1982 Usborne Publishing Ltd

Printed and bound in Great Britain

The name Usborne and the device are
Trade Marks of Usborne Publishing Ltd.

About this book

This book is for everyone learning French. By looking at the pictures, it will be easy to read and learn the words underneath them.

Masculine and Feminine Words

When you look at the words in French, you will see that most of them have **le, la, l'** or **les,** which means 'the', in front of them. When learning French, it is a good idea to learn the **le, la** or **l'** with each word. This is because all words in French, like car and train, as well as woman and man, are feminine or masculine. When you see **la,** the word is feminine. **Le** means the word is masculine. If the **le** or **la** comes before a word which begins with an **a, e, i, o, u,** or **h,** then the **le** or **la** usually becomes **l'.** **Les** can be either masculine or feminine but comes before words that are plural, that is, more than one, such as cars or trains.

Looking at the words

Some French words also have accents on the letters. These change the sound of the word. When the accent is on the last letter, that letter is then said. In French the last letter is not usually pronounced.

Saying the words

At the back of the book is a guide to pronouncing all the words on the pictures. This is to help you say all the words. But there are some sounds in French which are quite different from any sound in English. To say them as a French person would say them, you have to hear them spoken. Listen very carefully and then try to say them like that yourself. But if you say them as they are written in the pronunciation guide, a French person will understand you — even if your French accent is not quite perfect.

Can you find the dog?

On every picture across two pages there is a spotty dog to look for. Can you find it?

l'appartement

le parc de jeux

le balcon

l'hôpital

la statue

l'étalage de fleurs

le facteur

le kiosque à journeaux

la voiture de police

le réverbère

le trottoir

l'autopont

le parasol

le café

l'antenne

le cinéma

5

Les moyens de transport

le train

le pousse-pousse

le biplan

la camionnette

la bicyclette

le van

la voiture à cheval

la montgolfière

la voiture de sport

l'autobus

le camion transporteur

le pétrolier

le hang glider

le tank

le monorail

la remorque

le camion de déménagement

le tracteur

le camion

le tandem

la fusée

la roulotte

le parachute

le planeur

la moto

la voiture

le jumbo jet

le Concorde

l'hélicoptère

le dirigeable

le camion articulé

7

Sur l'eau

le filet

le panier à provisions

la rivière

le barrage

le canal

les joncs

le canoë

le pont

la canne à pêche

la ligne

le pêcheur

le transat

8

la péniche

le canard

le caneton

l'aqueduc

le radeau

l'écluse

le bateau
à moteur

le hors-bord

le canot
pneumatique

la jetée

le hangar à
bateaux

les roseaux

la péniche
d'habitation

la pagaie

le bouchon

le bateau de
plaisance

le cygne

le bateau à rames

la rame

9

Le port

le remorqueur

l'aéroglisseur

la grue

la borne d'amarrage

l'entrepôt

la bouée

les sacs de charbon

la caisse

le hublot

le sous-marin

10

le docker

la péniche

la cheminée

le bac à voitures

le container

le drapeau

le bateau de pêche

le pêcheur

le crochet

l'ancre

l'hydroglisseur

le réservoir

le filet

le marin

les marches

la voile

le pétrolier

le canot de sauvetage

la caisse d'emballage

le dragueur

la ceinture de sauvetage

le voilier

le paquebot

11

En montagne

le rocher

l'alpiniste

la corde

le mouflon

la chèvre

l'aigle

la cime

le piolet

12

le glacier

le lion de montagne

les skis

les pierres

le sapin

la caverne

la carte

le promeneur

le remonte-pente

la moraine

le sac à dos

la chute d'eau

l'ours   l'ourson

les bois

l'élan

la cabane de rondins

le bûcheron

les jumelles

la bûche

la scie

la hache

les chaussures de montagne

la forêt

13

l'âne

la selle

le rat
kangourou

le nomade

le chameau

le renard du
désert

le puits de
pétrole

l'autruche

l'antilope

le faucon

Dans le désert

la dune

le sable

le buisson d'épines

le puits

la tortue
du désert

la gazelle

la jeep

le palmier

la couverture

le crâne

le squelette

le serpent

le lièvre

le vautour

le lys
du désert

la
fourmi

la tente

l'oasis

le lézard

le scorpion

15

Le monde sous marin

le requin

l'aileron

le poisson

le masque

les bouteilles

le sable

les galets

l'éponge

le rocher

l'épave

le trésor

la corde

la grotte

l'étoile de mer

16

le crabe

le homard

le coquillage

les algues

l'huître

l'anémone
de mer

l'hippocampe

les bulles

le tentacule

les palmes

le plongeur

la pieuvre

la méduse

la combinaison
de plongée

17

le gorille

les bambous

la liane

le toucan

l'araignée

la flèche

le chasseur

la rainette

le papillon

18   le canoë

Dans la jungle

l'explorateur

le champignon

le jaguar

le chimpanzé

le caméléon

le serpent

la chauve-souris

le tapir

le singe

le crocodile

le galago

le paresseux

le perroquet

les empreintes

l'orchidée

l'oiseau-mouche

le tronc d'arbre

la passerelle de corde

la feuille

le fourmilier

19

Les pays froids

l'iceberg

la glace

le chien
de traîneau

le capuchon

le harpon

les lunettes

les glaçons

le bonhomme
de neige

la boule
de neige

l'igloo

l'avion à skis

le brise-glace

l'hirondelle
de mer

le phoque

le kayak

20

le renne

le morse

l'ours blanc

la neige

le tracteur
à chenilles

le traîneau

la baleine

le renard polaire

l'Esquimau

l'autochenille

le harfang des neiges

les raquettes

les moufles

le scooter
des neiges

21

Le carnaval

le bouclier

le tambour

le feu de joie

le cerceau

l'acrobate

la sorcière

le jongleur

la perruque

l'écharpe

le gland

la banderole

le plumet

le heaume

le masque

la lanterne

la cape

22

le feu d'artifice

la danseuse

les échasses

le balai

le clown

la boucle d'oreille

le dais

le char

la plume

les ballons

les éperons

la bougie

la flamme

la lance

le drapeau

23

La musique

le cor d'harmonie

la timbale

les baguettes de tambour

les castagnettes

le tambourin

le hautbois

le triangle

la guitare électrique

le pupitre à musique

le chef d'orchestre

l'orgue

le sitar

le concertina

l'accordéon

le xylophone

le basson

la trompette

l'harmonica

le violoncelle

24

le tuba

la balalaïka

le violon

l'archet

le saxophone

les cymbales

la harpe

la flûte à bec

les maracas

la cornemuse

la clochette

la guitare

le trombone

le banjo

la clarinette

la flûte traversière

la contrebasse

le piano

25

la brochette

la crêpe

la saucisse
chaude

la dinde

la pêche

les huîtres

les frites

la pomme

la glace

les saucisses
de Francfort

les spaghetti

Nourriture et boisson

la prune

le hamburger

le pain

le lait

la tomate

le café

26

les fraises

la bière

les sandwichs

le fromage

le poisson

la tourte

le thé

le vin

le gâteau

la charlotte

la poire

les cerises

la limonade

les escargots

le maïs

le riz

la salade

le paréo

les bottes

le kimono

le pantalon

le nœud
papillon

le caftan

la casquette

la soutane

le béret

Les vêtements

la cape

le feutre

le boléro

les babouches

le châle

le stetson

le bonnet

28

le survêtement

le chapeau
haut de forme

le poncho

le kilt

le sombrero

le sari

le fez

le voile

le costume
d'astronaute

l'habit

la queue-
de-pie

le turban

le pantalon
de cow-boy

les sandales

le smoking

le chapeau
chinois

les
sabots

29

Les choses qui poussent

le tabac

le riz

le blé

les dattes

les choux

les noix de coco

les tulipes

le coton

les raisins

le cacao

le thé

les ananas

les tournesols

le café

la canne à sucre

les bananes

le bois

31

Risques et périls

l'iceberg

les sables mouvants

le raz de marée

le volcan

le tremblement
de terre

la trombe

l'ouragan

l'incendie de forêt

l'avalanche

l'éclair

la tempête de neige

la tornade

la tempête de sable

l'inondation

33

Lieux d'habitations

la tente de bédouin

la hutte de terre

le bungalow

la maison-nid

le wigwam

la maison de Bornéo

la yourte

la péniche d'habitation

la péniche

la maison ronde

la hutte de feuilles

la cabane de joncs

le châlet

les appartements

le ranch

la maison de papier

le phare

la ferme

la roulotte de gitans

la maison caverne

la chaumière

la maison sur pilotis

le château

le fort

le sampan

la cabane de rondins

la maison de ville

35

Les animaux

l'orang-outang

le bison

le phascolome

l'ours koala

le ouistiti

le lion

le castor

le yak

la tortue géante

l'hippopotame

le raton laveur

le zèbre

le dauphin

le blaireau

l'éléphant

le tamias

le gibbon

le tigre

le lama

le panda géant

le putois

le gnou

le lémur

le porc-épic

le tatou

la hyène

le babouin

le kangourou

la girafe

le loup

le léopard

le rhinocéros

Monuments et sites connus

1 Neuschwanstein
   —Allemagne

2 La "Golden Gate"
   —États-Unis d'Amérique

3 La Tour de Pise
   —Italie

4 La Mosquée Bleue
   —Iran

5 L'Opéra de Sydney
   —Australie

7 L'Everest
   —Népal

6 Les Chutes du Niagara
   —États-Unis d'Amérique
   et Canada

8 La Tour Eiffel
38   —France

9 Stonehenge
   —Angleterre

10 La Cathédrale St. Basile
    —Russie

11   Le Taj Mahal
    —Inde

12   Une Pyramide et Le Sphinx
    —Égypte

13   Le Grand Canyon
    —États-Unis d'Amérique

14   La Tour de Londres
    —Angleterre

15   Le Parthénon
    —Grèce

16   La Statue de la Liberté
    —États-Unis
    d'Amérique

17   Le Colisée
    —Italie

18   Le Cap Kennedy
    —États-Unis d'Amérique

19   Le Temple du Paradis
    —Chine

Look at the map on the next two pages. Match up the numbers to find out
where the buildings and places are in the world.

La carte du monde

LE GROENLAND

L'OCÉAN ARCTIQUE

l'igloo

L'ALASKA

l'Esquimau

le bateau de pêche

LE CANADA

l'hovercraft

9 14

8

1

L'EUROP

6

3

LES ÉTATS-UNIS D'AMÉRIQUE

16

17

la fusée

le Concorde

15

2

13

18

L'OCÉAN ATLANTIQUE

L'AFRIC

L'AMÉRIQUE DU SUD

le paquebot

L'OCÉAN PACIFIQUE

Can you name the animals?

40   You can find them in this book.

le canot pneumatique

The numbers on the map show where the famous buildings and places are to be found. See pages 38 and 39.

la montgolfière

LA RUSSIE

L'OCÉAN PACIFIQUE

le raz de marée

19

7

LA CHINE

4

le puits
de pétrole

11

L'INDE

le sous-marin

le pétrolier

le jumbo jet

L'AUSTRALIE

l'hélicoptère

LA
NOUVELLE-ZÉLANDE

le brise-glace

L'ANTARCTIQUE

l'auto chenille

Index

On this page is the start of the alphabetical list of all the words in the pictures in this book. The French word comes first, then there is its pronunciation in *italics*, followed by the English translation.

There are some sounds in the French language which are quite different from any sounds in English. The pronunciation is a guide to help you say the French words correctly. They may look funny or strange. Just read them as if they are English words, except for these special rules:

g — is said like *g* in *g*ame.

j — is said like *s* in trea*s*ure

r — is made by a roll in the back of your mouth and sounds a little like gargling. When there is an *r* in the pronunciation guide, it is always said like this, except when it is in brackets, like this *(r)*

(n) — means that the *n* is not said but the vowel before it is nasalised. This means that you make the sound through your nose and your mouth at the same time. There are no sounds like this in English, so you have to hear someone say them before you can pronounce them correctly.

e — is said like the *'e'* in *'ten'* except when followed by *'r'*

er — sounds like the *'er'* in *'her'* except that the *'r'* is pronounced

e(r) — means that the *e* sounds like the *e* in *the* (not *thee*). The *r* is not said

ew — is a sound which we do not have in English. To make it, round your lips as if to say *oo*, then try and say *ee*

a — is said a little longer than *a* in c*a*t but not as long as the *a* in c*a*r

ay — is like *a* in d*a*te

French	Pronunciation	English
l'accordéon (f)	*la cor-day-o(n)*	accordion
l'acrobate (m)	*la-cro-bat*	acrobat
l'aéroglisseur (m)	*lair-o-glee-ser*	hovercraft
l'affiche (f)	*la-feesh*	advertisement
l'Afrique (f)	*la-freek*	Africa
l'aigle (m)	*lay-gl*	eagle
l'aileron (m)	*lel-ro(n)*	fin
l'Alaska (f)	*la-la-ska*	Alaska
les algues (f)	*lay-zalg*	seaweed
l'Allemagne (f)	*lal-man-ye(r)*	Germany
l'alpiniste (m)	*lal-pee-neest*	mountain climber
l'Amérique du Sud (f)	*la-may-reek dew sewd*	South America
l'ananas (m)	*la-na-na(s)*	pineapple
l'ancre (f)	*la(n)-cr*	anchor
l'âne (m)	*lan*	donkey
l'anemone de mer (f)	*la-nay-mo-n de(r) mair*	sea anemone
l'Angleterre (f)	*la(n)-gl-tair*	England
les animaux (m)	*lay-za-nee-mo*	animals
l'Antarctique (f)	*la(n)-tark-teek*	Antarctica
l'antenne (f)	*la(n)-ten*	aerial
l'antilope (f)	*la(n)-tee-lop*	antelope
l'appartement (m)	*la-par-te(r)-ma(n)*	flat
les appartements	*lay-za-par-te(r)-ma(n)*	flats
l'aqueduc (m)	*lack-dewk*	aqueduct
l'araignée (f)	*la-rayn-yay*	spider
l'arbre (m)	*lar-br*	tree
l'archet (m)	*lar-she*	bow (for violin)
l'arrêt d'autobus (m)	*la-re-doe-toe-bewce*	bus stop
l'Australie (f)	*loss-tra-lee*	Australia
l'autobus (m)	*lo-toe-bewce*	bus
l'autochenille (m)	*lo-toe-shen-ee*	snow cat
l'autopont (m)	*lo-toe-po(n)*	flyover
l'autruche (f)	*lo-trewsh*	ostrich
l'avalanche (f)	*la-va-la(n)sh*	avalanche
l'avion à skis (m)	*la-vee-o(n) a skee*	ski plane
les babouches (f)	*lay-ba-boosh*	slippers (eastern)
le babouin	*le(r) ba-bwa(n)*	baboon
le bac à voitures	*le(r) bac-a vwa-tewr*	car ferry
les baguettes de tambour (f)	*lay ba-get de(r) ta(n)-boor*	drumsticks
le balai	*le(r) ba-lay*	broomstick
la balalaïka	*la ba-la-la-ee-ka*	balalaika
le balcon	*le(r) bal-co(n)*	balcony
la baleine	*la ba-len*	whale
le ballon	*le(r) ba-lo(n)*	balloon
le bambou	*le(r) ba(n)-boo*	bamboo
la banane	*la ba-nan*	banana
la banderole	*la ba(n)-drol*	banner
le banjo	*le(r) ba(n)-jo*	banjo
le barrage	*le(r) ba-raj*	weir
le basson	*le(r) ba-so(n)*	bassoon
le bateau	*le(r) ba-toe*	boat
le bateau à moteur	*le(r) ba-toe a mo-ter*	motor boat
le bateau à rames	*le(r) ba-toe a ram*	rowing boat
le bateau de pêche	*le(r) ba-toe de(r) pesh*	fishing boat
le bateau de plaisance	*le(r) ba-toe de(r) play-za(n)ce*	cruiser (cabin cruiser)
le bâton	*le(r) ba-to(n)*	baton
le béret	*le(r) bay-ray*	beret
la bicyclette	*la bee-see-clet*	bicycle
la bière	*la bee-air*	beer
le biplan	*le(r) bee-pla(n)*	bi-plane
le bison	*le(r) bee-son*	bison

French	Pronunciation	English
le blaireau	le(r) blay-ro	badger
le blé	le(r) blay	wheat
le bois	le(r) bwa	timber
les bois (m)	lay bwa	antlers
la boisson	la bwa-so(n)	drink
le boléro	le(r) bo-lay-ro	bolero
le bonhomme de neige	le(r) bon-om de(r) nej	snowman
le bonnet	le(r) bon-nay	bonnet
la borne d'amarrage	la born da-ma-raj	bollard
la botte	la bot	boot
le bouchon	le(r) boo-sho(n)	float
la boucle d'oreille	le boo-cl do-ray	earring
le bouclier	le(r) boo-clee-ay	shield
la bouée	la boo-ay	buoy
la bougie	la boo-jee	candle
la boule de neige	la bool de(r) nej	snowball
les bouteilles (f)	lay boo-tay	aqualung
le brise-glace	le(r) breez-glass	ice breaker
les brochettes (f)	lay bro-shet	shish kebab
la bûche	la bewsh	log
le bûcheron	le(r) bewsh-ro(n)	lumberjack
le buisson d'épines	le(r) bwee-so(n) day-peen	thornbush
le bungalow	le(r) ba(n)-ga-lo	bungalow
la cabane de joncs	la ca-ban de(r) jo(n)	reed hut
la cabane de rondins	la ca-ban de(r) ro(n)-da(n)	log cabin
le cacao	le(r) ca-ca-o	cocoa
le café	le(r) ca-fay	coffee, café
le caftan	le(r) kaf-ta(n)	kaftan
la caisse	la kess	box
la caisse d'emballage	la kess da(n)-ba-laj	crate
le caméléon	le(r) ca-may-lay-o(n)	chameleon
le camion	le(r) ca-mee-o(n)	lorry
le camion articulé	le(r) cam-mee-o(n)ar-tee-kew-lay	juggernaut
le camion de déménagement	le(r) ca-mee-o(n) de(r) day-may-naj-ma(n)	removal van
le camion transporteur	le(r) ca-mee-o(n) tra(n)-spor-ter	transporter
la camionnette	la ca-mee-on-et	van
le Canada	le(r) ca-na-da	Canada
le canal	le(r) ca-nal	canal
le canard	le(r) ca-nar	duck
le caneton	le(r) can-to(n)	duckling
la canne à pêche	la can a pesh	fishing rod
la canne à sucre	la can a sew-cr	sugar cane
le canoë	le(r) ca-no-ay	canoe
le canot de sauvetage	le(r) ca-no de(r) sov-taj	lifeboat
le canot pneumatique	le(r) ca-no pne(r)-ma-teek	rubber dinghy
le Cap Kennedy	le(r) cap ke-ne(r)-dee	Cape Kennedy
la cape	la cap	cape
le capuchon	le(r) ca-poosh-o(n)	hood
le carnaval	le(r) car-na-val	carnival
la carte	la cart	map
la carte du monde	la cart dew mo(n)d	map of the world
la caserne de pompiers	la ca-sairn de(r) po(n) pee-ay	fire station
la casquette	la cass-ket	cap
les castagnettes (f)	lay cass-tan-yet	castanets
le castor	le(r) cass-tor	beaver
la Cathédrale St Basile	la ca-tay-dral sa(n)ba-zeel	St Basil's Cathedral
la caverne	la ca-vairn	cave
la ceinture de sauvetage	la sa(n)-tewr de(r) so-ve-tahj	lifebelt
le cerceau	le(r) sair-so	hoop
la cerise	la se(r)-ees	cherry
les cerises (f)	lay se(r)-reez	cherries
le châle	le(r) shall	shawl
le chalet	le(r) sha-le	chalet
le chameau	le(r) sha-mo	camel
le champignon	le(r) sha(n)-pee n-yon	mushroom
le chapeau	le(r) sha-po	hat
le chapeau chinois	le(r) sha-po sheen-wa	coolie hat
le chapeau haute de forme	le(r) sha-po o de(r) form	top hat
le char	le(r) shar	carriage (at carnival time)
la charlotte	la shar-lot	jelly
le chasseur	le(r) sha-ser	hunter
le château	le(r) sha-toe	castle
la chaumière	la sho-mee-air	cottage
les chaussures de montagne (f)	lay sho-sewr de(r) mo(n)-tan-ye(r)	climbing boots
la chauve-souris	la shoav-soo-ree	bat
le chef d'orchestre	le(r) shef-dor-kess-tr	conductor
la cheminée	lc she(r)-mee-nay	chimney
la chèvre	la she-vr	goat
le chien de traîneau	le(r) shee-a(n) de(r) tray-no	husky dog
le chimpanzé	le(r) sha(n)-pa(n)-zay	chimpanzee
la Chine	la sheen	China
les choses qui poussent (f)	lay showz kee pooce	things which grow
le chou	le(r) shoo	cabbage
la chute d'eau	la shewt doe	waterfall
les Chutes du Niagara (f)	lay shewt dew nee-a-ga-ra	Niagara Falls
la cime	la seem	peak
le cinéma	le(r) see-nay-ma	cinema
la clarinette	la cla-ree-net	clarinet
la clochette	la clo-shet	hand-bell
le clown	le(r) cloon	clown
le coléoptère	le(r) co-lay-op-tair	beetle
le Colisée	le(r) co-lee-say	Colosseum
la combinaison de plongée	la co(n)-bee-nay-zo(n) de(r) plo(n)j-ay	wetsuit
la concertina	la co(n)-sair-tee-na	concertina
le Concorde	le(r) co(n)-cord	Concorde
le container	le(r) co(n)-tay-nair	container
la contrebasse	la co(n)-tr-bass	double bass
le coquillage	le(r) cock-ee-aj	shell
le cor d'harmonie	le(r) cor dar-mo-nee	French horn
la corde	la cord	rope
la cornemuse	la cor-ne(r)-mewz	bagpipes
le costume d'astronaute	le(r) coss-tewm dass-tron-oat	space suit

le coton	le(r) cot-o(n)	cotton
la couverture	la coo-vair-tewr	blanket
le crabe	le(r) crab	crab
le crâne	le(r) cran	skull
la crêpe	la crep	pancake
le crochet	le(r)cro shay	hook
le crocodile	le(r) cro-co-d-eel	crocodile
le cygne	le(r) seen-ye(r)	swan
les cymbales (f)	lay sa(n)-bal	cymbals
le dais	le(r) day	canopy
dans le désert	da(n) le(r) day-zair	in the desert
dans la jungle	da(n) la je(r)(n)-gl	in the jungle
la danseuse	la da(n)-se(r)z	dancer (female)
les dattes (f)	lay dat	dates
le dauphin	le(r) doe-fa(n)	dolphin
le désert	le(r) day-zair	desert
la dinde	la da(n)d	turkey
le dirigeable	le(r) dee-ree-ja-bl	airship
le docker	le(r) dock-er	docker
le dragueur	le(r) dra-ger	dredger
le drapeau	le(r) dra-po	flag
la dune	la dewn	sand dune
l'eau (f)	lo	water
l'écharpe (f)	lay-sharp	scarf or muffler
les échasses (f)	lay-zay-shass	stilts
l'éclair (m)	lay-clair	lightning
l'écluse (f)	lay-clewz	lock
l'église (f)	lay-gleez	church
l'Égypte (f)	lay-jeet	Egypt
l'élan (m)	lay-la(n)	moose
l'éléphant (m)	lay-lay-fa(n)	elephant
en montagne	a(n) mo(n)-tan-ye(r)	in the mountains
en ville	a(n) veel	in the city
les empreintes (f)	lays-a(n)-pran-te(r)	footprints or tracks
l'entrepôt (m)	la(n)-tr-po	warehouse
l'épave (f)	lay-pav	wreck
les éperons (m)	lay-zay-pay-ro(n)	spurs
l'éponge (f)	lay-po(n)j	sponge
l'escargot (m)	less-car-go	snail
l'Esquimau (m)	less-kee-mo	Eskimo
l'étalage de fleurs (m)	lay ta-laj de(r) fler	flower stall
les États-Unis d'Amérique (m)	lay zay-ta ew-nee da-may-reek	United States of America
l'étoile de mer (f)	lay-twal de(r) mair	starfish
l'Europe (f)	ler-op	Europe
l'Everest (m)	lev-e(r)-est	Mount Everest
l'explorateur	lex-plo-ra-ter	explorer
le facteur	le(r) fack-ter	postman
le faucon	le(r) fo-co(n)	falcon or hawk
la ferme	la fairm	farm house
le feu d'artifice	le(r) fe(r) dar-tee-feece	fireworks
le feu de joie	le(r) fe(r) de(r) jwa	bonfire
la feuille	la fe(r)-ye(r)	leaf
le feutre	le(r) fe(r)-tr	hat
les feux de signalisation (m)	lay fe(r) de(r) see-nyal-ee-sa-seeo(n)	traffic lights
le fez	le(r) fez	fez
le filet	le(r)fee le	net
la flamme	la flam	flame
la flèche	la flesh	arrow
la flûte à bec	la flewt a bek	recorder
la flûte traversière	la flewt tra-vair-see-air	flute
la forêt	la fo-ray	forest
le fort	le(r) for	fort
la fourmi	la foor-mee	ant
le fourmilier	le(r) foor-mee-lee-ay	anteater
la fraise	la frayz	strawberry
la France	la fra(n)ce	France
les frites (f)	lay freet	chips
le fromage	le(r) fro-maj	cheese
la fusée	la few-zay	rocket
le galago	le(r) ga-la-go	bushbaby
le galet	le(r) ga-lay	pebble
le garage	le(r) ga-raj	garage
le garçon de café	le(r) gar-so(n) de(r) ca-fay	waiter
le gâteau	le(r) ga-toe	gateau or cake
la gazelle	la ga-zell	gazelle
le gibbon	le(r) jee-bo(n)	gibbon
la girafe	la jee-raff	giraffe
la glace	la glass	ice cream
le glacier	le(r) gla-see-ay	glacier
le gland	le(r) gla(n)	tassel
le gnou	le(r) noo	gnu
la Golden Gate	la gol-den gate	Golden Gate Bridge
le gorille	le(r) go-ree-ye(r)	gorilla
le Grand Canyon	le(r) gra(n) can-yon	Grand Canyon
la Grèce	la gress	Greece
le Groenland	le(r) gro-en-land	Greenland
la grotte	la grot	cave
la grue	la grew	crane
la guitare	la gee-tar	guitar
la guitare électrique	la gee-tar ay-leck-treek	electric guitar
l'habit de religieuse	la-bee de(r) ray-lee-jee-ers	nun's habit
la hâche	la ash	axe
le hamburger	le(r) am-bu(r)-gair	hamburger
le hang glider	le(r)a(n)-glee-der	hang glider
le hangar à bateaux	le(r) a(n)-gar a ba-toe	boat house
le harfang des neiges	le(r) ar-fa(n) day nej	snowy owl
l'harmonica (m)	lar-mo-nee-ca	mouth organ
la harpe (f)	la arp	harp
le harpon	le(r) ar-po(n)	harpoon
le hautbois	le(r) o bwa	oboe
l'hélicoptère (m)	lay-lee-cop-tair	helicopter
le heaume	le(r) o-m	helmet

l'hippocampe (m)	*lee-po-ca(n)p*	sea horse
l'hippopotame (m)	*lee-po-po-tam*	hippopotamus
l'hirondelle de mer (f)	*lee-ro(n) dell de(r) mair*	tern
le homard	*le(r) om-ar*	lobster
l'hôpital (m)	*lop-ee-tal*	hospital
le hors-bord	*le(r) or-bor*	outboard motor
le hot-dog	*le(r) hot-dog*	hotdog
l'hôtel	*lo-tell*	hotel
le hublot	*ler ew-blo*	porthole
l'huître	*lwee-tr*	oyster
les huîtres (f)	*lay wee-tr*	oysters
la hutte de feuilles	*la,ewt de(r) fe(r)-ye(r)*	grass hut
la hutte de terre	*la ewt de(r) tair*	mud hut
l'hydroglisseur	*lee-dro-glee-ser*	hydrofoil
la hyène	*la ee-en*	hyena
l'iceberg (m)	*leece-bairg*	iceberg
l'igloo (m)	*lee-gloo*	igloo
l'incendie de forêt (m)	*la(n)-sa(n)-dee de(r) fo-ray*	forest fire
l'Inde (f)	*la(n)d*	India
l'inondation (f)	*lee-no(n)-da-see-o(n)*	flood
les instruments de musique (m)	*lay za(n)-stroo-ma(n)de(r) mew-zeek*	musical instruments
L'Iran (m)	*leer-ran*	Iran
l'Italie (f)	*lee-ta-lee*	Italy
le jaguar	*le(r) ja-goo-ar*	jaguar
le jardin public	*le(r) jar-da(n) poo-bleek*	park
la jeep (f)	*la jeep*	jeep
la jetée	*la je(r)-tay*	jetty
les joncs (m)	*lay jo(n)*	bulrushes
le jongleur	*le(r) jo(n)-gler*	juggler
le jumbo jet	*le(r) ja(n)-bo jet*	jumbo jet
les jumelles (f)	*lay jew-mell*	binoculars
la jungle	*la je(r)(n) -gl*	jungle
le kangourou	*le(r) ka(n)-goo-roo*	kangaroo
le kayak	*le(r) ka-yak*	kayak
le kilt	*le(r) keelt*	kilt
le kimono	*le(r) kee-mo-no*	kimono
le kiosque à journaux	*le(r) kee-osk a joor-no*	newspaper stand
le lait	*le(r) lay*	milk
le lama	*le(r) la-ma*	llama
le lampion	*le(r) la(n)-pee-o(n)*	lantern
la lance	*la la(n)ce*	spear
la lanterne	*la la(n)-tairn*	lantern
le lémur	*le(r) lay-mewr*	lemur
le léopard	*le(r) lay-o-par*	leopard
le lézard	*le(r) lay-zar*	lizard
la liane	*la lee-an*	creeper
lieux d'habitation (m)	*lye(r) da-bee-tasee-o(n)*	houses and homes
le lièvre	*le(r) lee-evr*	hare
la ligne	*la leen-ye(r)*	line
la limonade	*la lee-mo-nad*	lemonade
le lion	*le(r) lee-o(n)*	lion
le lion de montagne	*le(r) lee-o(n) de(r) mo(n)-tan-ye(r)*	mountain lion
le loup	*le(r) loo*	wolf
les lunettes (f)	*lay lew-net*	glasses
le lys du désert	*le(r) leece dew day-zair*	desert lily
le magasin	*le(r) ma-ga-zan*	shop
le maïs	*le(r) ma-eece*	corn
la maison	*la may-zo(n)*	house
la maison caverne	*la may-zo(n) ca-vairn*	cave house
la maison de Bornéo	*la may-zo(n) de(r) bor-nay-o*	house in Borneo (longhouse)
la maison de papier	*la may-zo(n) de(r) pa-pee-ay*	paper house
la maison ronde	*la may-zo(n) ro(n)d*	dome house
la maison de ville	*la may-zo(n) de(r) veel*	terraced house
la maison-nid	*lay may-zo(n) nee*	tree house
la maison-sur-pilotis	*la may-zo(n)-sewr-pee-lo-tee*	stilt house
les maracas	*lay ma-ra-cas*	maracas
les marches (f)	*lay marsh*	steps
le marin	*le(r) ma-ra(n)*	sailor
le masque	*le(r) mask*	mask
la méduse	*la may-dewz*	jellyfish
le monde	*le(r) mo(n)d*	world
le monde sous-marin	*le(r) mo(n)d soo-ma-ra(n)*	under the sea
le monorail	*le(r) mo-no-rye*	monorail
la montagne	*la mo(n)-tan-ye(r)*	mountain
la montgolfière	*la mo(n)-gol-fee-air*	hot air balloon
monuments et sites connus (m)	*mo-new-ma(n) ay seet co-new*	famous buildings and places
la moraine	*la mo-ren*	boulder
le morse	*le(r) morce*	walrus
la Mosquée Bleue	*la mo-skay ble(r)*	Blue Mosque
le moteur	*le(r) mo-ter*	motor or engine
la moto	*la mo-to*	motorcycle
les moufles (f)	*lay moo-fl*	mittens
le mouflon	*le(r) moo-flo(n)*	mountain sheep
les moyens de transport	*lay mwa-yen de(r)-tra(n)-spor*	transport
la musique	*la mew-zeek*	music
la neige	*la nej*	snow
le Népal	*le(r) nay-pal*	Nepal
Neuschwanstein	*noysh-van-shtine*	Ludwig's castle
le noeud papillon	*le(r) ne(r) pa-pee-yon*	bow tie
la noix de coco	*la nwa de(r) co-co*	coconut
le nomade	*le(r) no-mad*	nomad
la nourriture	*la noo-ree-tewr*	food
nourriture et boisson	*noo-ree-tewr ay bwa-so(n)*	food and drink
la Nouvelle-Zélande	*la noo-vell zay-la(n)d*	New Zealand

French	Pronunciation	English
l'oasis (f)	lo-az-eece	oasis
l'Océan Arctique (m)	lo-say-a(n) arc-teek	Arctic Ocean
l'Océan Atlantique (m)	lo-say-a(n) at-la(n)-teek	Atlantic Ocean
l'Océan Pacifique (m)	lo-say-a(n) pasee-feek	Pacific Ocean
l'oiseau-mouche (m)	lwa-zo moosh	humming-bird
l'Opéra de Sydney (m)	lo-pay-ra de(r) seed-nay	The Sydney Opera House
l'orang-outang (m)	lo-ra(n) oo-ta(n)	orang-utan
l'orchidée	lor-shee-day	orchid
l'orgue (m)	lorg	organ
le ouistiti	le(r) wee-stee-tee	marmoset
l'ouragan (m)	loo-ra-ga(n)	hurricane
l'ours (m)	loorce	bear
l'ours blanc (m)	loorce bla(n)	polar bear
l'ours koala (m)	loorce ko-a-la	koala bear
l'ourson (m)	loor-so(n)	bear cub
la pagaie	la pa-gay	paddle
le pain	le(r) pa(n)	bread
les palmes (f)	lay palm	flippers
le palmier	le(r) palm-ee-ay	palm tree
le panda géant	le(r) pa(n)-da jay-a(n)	giant panda
le panier à provisions	le(r) pa-nee-ay a pro-vee-zee-o(n)	hamper
le panneau indicateur	le(r) pa-no a(n)-dee-ca-ter	road sign
le pantalon	le(r) pa(n)-ta-lo(n)	trousers
le pantalon de cow-boy	le(r) pa(n)-ta-lo(n) de(r) cow-boy	chaps
le papillon	le(r) pa-pee-yon	butterfly
le paquebot	le(r) pack-bo	liner
le parachute	le(r) pa-ra-shewt	parachute
le parasol	le(r) pa-ra-sol	umbrella
le parc de jeux	le(r) parc de(r) je(r)	playground
le paréo	le(r) pa-ray-o	grass skirt
le paresseux	le(r) pa-ra-se(r)	sloth
le Parthénon	le(r) par-tay-no(n)	Parthenon
le passage-clouté	le(r) pa-saj cloo-tay	crossing
la passerelle de corde	la pass-rell de(r)-cord	rope bridge
les pays froids (m)	lay pay frwa	cold lands
la pêche	la pesh	peach
la pêche à la ligne	la pesh a la leen-ye(r)	fishing
le pêcheur	le(r) pesh-er	fisherman
la péniche	la pay-neesh	barge
la péniche d'habitation	la pay-neesh da-bee-ta-see-o(n)	houseboat
le péril	le(r) pay-reel	danger
le perroquet	le(r) pay-rock-ay	parrot
la perruque	la pay-rewk	wig
le pétrole	le(r) pay-troll	oil (fuel)
le pétrolier	le(r) pay-troll-ee-ay	oiltanker
le phare	le(r) far	lighthouse
le phascolome	le(r) fa-sco-lom	wombat
le phoque	le(r) fock	seal
le piano	le(r) pee-a-no	piano
la pierre	la pee-air	stone
la pieuvre	la pee-e(r)-vr	octopus
le piolet	le(r) pee-o-lay	ice axe
le planeur	le(r) pla-ner	glider
le plongeur	le(r) plo(n)-jer	diver
la plume	la plewm	feather
le plumet	le(r) plew-may	plume
la poire	la pwar	pear
le poisson	le(r) pwa-so(n)	fish
la police	la po-leece	police
la pomme	la pom	apple
le pompier	le(r) po(n)-pee-ay	fireman
le poncho	le(r) po(n)-sho	poncho
le pont	le(r) po(n)	bridge
le porc-épic	le(r) por-cay-peek	porcupine
le port	le(r) por	harbour
le pousse-pousse	le(r) pooce-pooce	rickshaw
le promeneur	le(r) prom-ner	walker
la prune	la prewn	plum
le puits	le(r) pwee	well
le puits de pétrole	le(r) pwee de(r) pay-trol	oilwell
le pupitre à musique	le(r) pew-pee-tra-mew-zeek	music stand
le putois	le(r) pew-twa	skunk
la Pyramide	la pee-ra-meed	pyramid
la queue-de-pie	la ke(r) de (r) pee	tail coat
le radeau	le(r) ra-do	raft
la rainette	la ren-et	tree frog
les raisins (m)	lay ray-sa(n)	grapes
la rame	la ram	oar
le ranch	le(r) ra(n)sh	ranch house
les raquettes (f)	lay ra-ket	snow shoes
le rat kangourou	le(r) ra ka(n)-goo-roo	kangaroo rat
le raton laveur	le(r) ra-to(n) la-ver	racoon
le raz de marée	le(r) ra de(r) ma-ray	tidal wave
le remonte-pente	le(r) re(r)-mo(n)t pa(n)t	ski lift
la remorque	la re(r)-mork	trailer
le remorqueur	le(r)re(r)-mor-ker	tug
le renard polaire	le(r) re(r)-nar po-lair	arctic fox
le renard du désert	le(r) re(r)-nar dew day-zair	desert fox
le renne	le(r) ren	reindeer
le requin	le(r) re(r)-ka(n)	shark
le réservoir	le(r) ray-zay-vwar	tank or storage tank
le réverbère	le(r) ray-vair-bair	street light
le rhinocéros	le(r) ree-noss-ay-ross	rhinoceros
la rivière	la ree-vee-air	river
le riz	le(r) ree	rice
le rocher	le(r) rosh-ay	rock
le roseau	le(r) roz-o	reed
la roulotte	la roo-lot	caravan
la roulotte de gitans (f)	la roo-lot de(r) jee-ta(n)	gypsy caravan
la Russie	la rew-see	Russia
le sable	le(r) sa-bl	sand
les sables mouvants (m)	lay sa-bl moo-va(n)	quicksand
les sabots (m)	lay sa-bo	clogs
le sac à dos	le(r) sa-ca-doe	haversack

les sacs (de charbon) (m)	*lay sack de(r) shar-bo(n)*	sacks (of coal)		la Tour de Londres	*la toor de(r) lo(n)-dr*	Tower of London
la salade	*la sa-lad*	salad		la Tour de Pise	*la toor de(r) peez*	Leaning Tower of Pisa
le sampan	*le(r) sa(n) pa(n)*	sampan				
les sandales (f)	*lay sa(n)-dal*	sandals		la Tour Eiffel	*la toor ee-fell*	Eiffel Tower
le sandwich	*le(r) sa(n)d-weetsh*	sandwich		le tournesol	*le(r) toor-ne(r)-sol*	sunflower
le sapin	*le(r) sa-pan*	fir tree		la tourte	*la toort*	pie
le sari	*le(r) sa-ree*	sari		le tracteur	*le(r) track-ter*	tractor
la saucisse de francfort	*la so-seece de(r) fra(n)c-for*	frankfurter		le train	*le(r) tra(n)*	train
le saxophone	*le(r) sax-o-fon*	saxophone		le traineau	*le(r) tre-no*	sledge
la scie	*la see*	saw		le transat	*le(r) tra(n)-sa*	deck chair
le scorpion	*le(r) scor-pee-o(n)*	scorpion		le tremblement de terre	*le(r) tra(n)-bl-ma(n) de(r) tair*	earthquake
la selle	*la sell*	saddle		le trésor	*le(r) tray-zor*	treasure chest
le serpent	*le(r) sair-pa(n)*	snake				
le singe	*le(r) sa(n)j*	monkey		le triangle	*le(r) tree-a(n)gl*	triangle
le sitar	*le(r) see-tar*	sitar		la trombe	*la tro(n)b*	waterspout
les skis (m)	*lay skee*	skis		le trombone	*le(r) tro(n)-bon*	trombone
le smoking	*le(r) smo-keen(g)*	tuxedo, dinner jacket		la trompette	*la tro(n)-pet*	trumpet
				le tronc d'arbre	*le(r) tro(n) dar-br*	tree trunk
la snowmobile	*la snow-mo-beel*	snowmobile		le trottoir	*le(r) tro-twar*	pavement
le sombrero	*le(r) so(n)-bray-ro*	sombrero		le tuba	*le(r) tew-ba*	tuba
la sorcière	*la sor-see-air*	witch		la tulipe	*la tew-leep*	tulip
le sous-marin	*ler soo ma-ran*	submarine		le turban	*le(r) tewr-ba(n)*	turban
la soutane	*la soo-tan*	cassock				
les spaghetti (m)	*lay spa-ge-tee*	spaghetti		l'usine (f)	*lew-zeen*	factory
le Sphinx	*le(r) sfa(n)ks*	Sphinx				
le squelette	*le(r) ske(r)-let*	skeleton		le van	*le(r) van*	horse-box
la statue	*la sta-tew*	statue		le vautour	*le(r) vo-toor*	vulture
la Statue de la Liberté	*la sta-tew de(r) la leeb air tay*	Statue of Liberty		les vêtements (m)	*lay vet-ma(n)*	clothes
le stetson	*le(r) stet-so(n)*	stetson		la ville	*la veel*	town or city
Stonehenge	*ston-enj*	Stonehenge		le vin	*le(r) va(n)*	wine
sur l'eau	*sewr lo*	on the water		le violon	*le(r) vee-o-lo(n)*	violin
le survêtement	*le(r) sewr-vet-ma(n)*	tracksuit		le violoncelle	*le(r) vee-o-lo(n)-sell*	cello
				la voile	*la vwal*	sail
				le voile	*le(r) vwal*	yashmak
le tabac	*le(r) ta-back*	tobacco		le voilier	*le(r) vwal-yay*	sailing dinghy or boat
le Taj Mahal	*le(r) taj ma-al*	Taj Mahal				
le tambour	*le(r) ta(n)-boor*	drum		la voiture	*la vwa-tewr*	car
le tambourin	*le(r) ta(n)-boor-a(n)*	tambourine		la voiture à cheval	*la vwa-tewr a she(r)-val*	horse and cart
le tamias	*le(r) ta-mee-a*	chipmunk		la voiture de police	*la vwa-tewr de(r) po-leece*	police car
le tandem	*le(r) ta(n) dem*	tandem				
le tank	*le(r) ta(n)*	tank		la voiture de pompiers	*la vwa-tewr de(r) po(n)-pee-ay*	fire engine
le tapir	*le(r) ta-peer*	tapir				
le tatou	*le(r) ta-too*	armadillo		la voiture de sport	*la vwa-tewr de(r) spor*	sports car
la tempête de neige	*la ta(n)-pet de(r) nej*	blizzard		le volcan	*le(r) vol ca(n)*	volcano
la tempête de sable	*la ta(n)-pet de(r) sa-bl*	sandstorm				
le Temple du Paradis	*le(r) ta(m)-pl dew pa-ra-dee*	The Temple of Heaven		le wigwam	*le(r) wig-wam*	wigwam
la tentacule	*la ta(n)-ta-cewl*	tentacle				
la tente	*la ta(n)t*	tent		le xylophone	*le(r) ksee-lo-fon*	xylophone
la tente de bédouin	*la ta(n)t de(r) bay-dew-a(n)*	Bedouin tent				
le thé	*le(r) tay*	tea		le yak	*le(r) yak*	yak
le tigre	*le(r) tee-gr*	tiger		la yourte	*la yoort*	yurt
le timbale	*la ta(n)-bal*	kettle drum				
la tomate	*la to-mat*	tomato		le zèbre	*le(r) zay-br*	zebra
la tornade	*la tor-nad*	tornado				
la tortue du desert	*la tor-too dew day-zair*	desert turtle				
la tortue géante	*la tor-too-jay-a(n)t*	tortoise				
le toucan	*le(r) too-can*	toucan				